ISBN 978-0-265-79226-1
PIBN 10966699

1 MONTH OF
FREE
READING

at

www.ForgottenBooks.com

By purchasing this book you are eligible for one month membership to ForgottenBooks.com, giving you unlimited access to our entire collection of over 1,000,000 titles via our web site and mobile apps.

To claim your free month visit:
www.forgottenbooks.com/free966699

English
Français
Deutsche
Italiano
Español
Português

www.forgottenbooks.com

Mythology Photography **Fiction**
Fishing Christianity **Art** Cooking
Essays Buddhism Freemasonry
Medicine **Biology** Music **Ancient
Egypt** Evolution Carpentry Physics
Dance Geology **Mathematics** Fitness
Shakespeare **Folklore** Yoga Marketing
Confidence Immortality Biographies
Poetry **Psychology** Witchcraft
Electronics Chemistry History **Law**
Accounting **Philosophy** Anthropology
Alchemy Drama Quantum Mechanics
Atheism Sexual Health **Ancient History**
Entrepreneurship Languages Sport
Paleontology Needlework Islam
Metaphysics Investment Archaeology
Parenting Statistics Criminology
Motivational

Department of Agriculture

Forest Service

Intermountain Research Station

Resource Bulletin ^
INT-43

Colorado's Southern Front Range: Forest Statistics for State and Private Land, 1983

Roger C. Conner
William T. Pawley

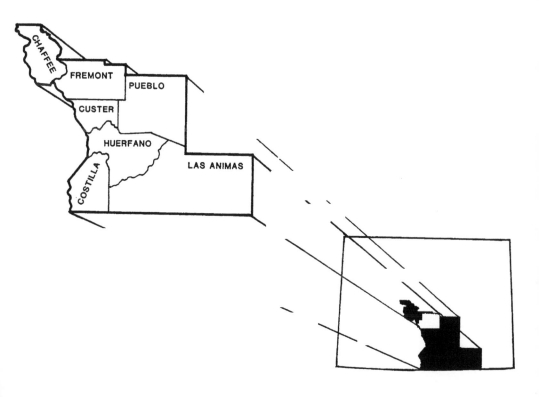

THE AUTHORS

ROGER C. CONNER is a forester with the Forest Survey research work unit at the Intermountain Research Station in Ogden, UT. His primary area of responsibility is in resource analysis. He holds a B.S. degree in forestry from Virginia Polytechnic Institute and State University. He began his Forest Service career with the Intermountain Station in 1980.

WILLIAM T. PAWLEY is a forester with the Forest Survey research work unit at the Intermountain Research Station in Ogden, UT. His primary area of responsibility is in data collection. He holds a B.S. degree in forestry from Northern Arizona University. He has been with the Intermountain Station since 1980.

ACKNOWLEDGMENTS

This report is the result of the combined efforts of numerous people on the Forest Survey staff. In addition to the photo interpretation and field crews, several individuals played key roles in the reduction of basic data into information describing the extent, nature, and condition of the forest resources in Colorado: Dennis Collins supervised the data collection; Sharon Woudenberg and Shirley Waters compiled the data and made summaries; and Susan Brown and Velma Sterrett transformed the data summaries into tables of information. Also, acknowledgment is given to the Colorado State Forest Service for its cooperation and assistance in collecting the inventory data. And we extend a special note of gratitude to the private land owners who allowed the field crews access to the sample locations on their properties.

RESEARCH SUMMARY

Presents land area, timberland timber inventory, and growth and counties in Colorado's southern and statistical tables are based lected from 1982 and 1983 and resources.

CONTENTS

Introduction . . . .
Highlights . . . .
  Area . . . .
  Inventory . . . .
  Components of Change . . . . .
How the Inventory was Conduct
  Prefield . . . .
  Field . . . .
  Compilation . . . .
Data Reliability . . . .
Terminology and Data Tables . .
Terminology . . . .
References . . . .

Figures

  1. Counties covered by this
  2. Distribution of land area i
     Front Range by owner gr

August 1987
Intermountain Research Station
324 25th Street
Ogden, UT 84401

Forest Survey Tables   Page

1. Area of State and privately owned forest land with percent standard error in Colorado's southern Front Range, 1983 . . . .   *7*

2. Net volume, net annual growth, and annual mortality of growing stock and sawtimber on State and privately owned timberland with percent standard error in Colorado's southern Front Range *7*

3. Total land and water area by ownership class in Colorado's southern Front Range, 1983   8

4. Total land area on State and privately owned land by major land class and ownership class in Colorado's southern Front Range, 1983   8

5. Area of forest land on State and privately owned land by forest type, ownership class, and land class in Colorado's southern Front Range, 1983   9

6. Cubic feet of net volume in trees on State and privately owned forest land by species and ownership class in Colorado's southern Front Range, 1983   10

7. Cubic feet of net annual growth in trees on State and privately owned forest land by species and ownership class in Colorado's southern Front Range, 1982   10

8. Cubic feet of annual mortality in trees on State and privately owned forest land by species and ownership class in Colorado's southern Front Range, 1982   11

9. Area of State and privately owned timberland by forest type, stand-size class, and productivity class in Colorado's southern Front Range, 1983   12

10. Area of State owned timberland by forest type, stand-size class, and productivity class in Colorado's southern Front Range, 1983   14

11. Area of nonindustrial privately owned timberland by forest type, stand-size class, and productivity class in Colorado's southern Front Range, 1983   16

12. Area of State and privately owned timberland by stand volume and ownership class in Colorado's southern Front Range, 1983   18

13. Area of State and privately owned timberland by forest type and area condition class in Colorado's southern Front Range, 1983   18

14. Number of growing-stock trees on State and privately owned timberland by species and diameter class in Colorado's southern Front Range, 1983   19

15. Number of cull and salvable dead trees on State and privately owned timberland by ownership class, and softwoods and hardwoods in Colorado's southern Front Range, 1983   20

16. Net volume of growing stock on State and privately owned timberland by ownership class, forest type, and stand-size class in Colorado's southern Front Range, 1983   21

17. Net volume of sawtimber (International ¼-inch rule) on State and privately owned timberland by ownership class, forest type, and stand-size class in Colorado's southern Front Range, 1983   22

18. Net volume of sawtimber (Scribner rule) on State and privately owned timberland by ownership class, forest type, and stand-size class in Colorado's southern Front Range, 1983   23

19. Net volume of growing stock on State and privately owned timberland by ownership class and species in Colorado's southern Front Range, 1983   24

20. Net volume of sawtimber (International ¼-inch rule) on State and privately owned timberland by ownership class and species in Colorado's southern Front Range, 1983   24

21. Net volume of sawtimber (Scribner rule) on State and privately owned timberland by ownership class and species in Colorado's southern Front Range, 1983   25

22. Net volume of growing stock on State and privately owned timberland by species and diameter class in Colorado's southern Front Range, 1983   26

23. Net volume of sawtimber (International ¼-inch rule) on State and privately owned timberland by species and diameter class in Colorado's southern Front Range, 1983   27

24. Net volume of sawtimber (Scribner rule) on State and privately owned timberland by species and diameter class in Colorado's southern Front Range, 1983   28

25. Net volume of timber on State and privately owned timberland by class of timber, and softwoods and hardwoods in Colorado's southern Front Range, 1983   29

26. Net volume of growing stock on State and privately owned timberland by forest type and species in Colorado's southern Front Range, 1983   29

27. Net volume of sawtimber (International ¼-inch rule) on State and privately owned timberland by forest type and species in Colorado's southern Front Range, 1983   30

28. Net volume of sawtimber (Scribner rule) on State and privately owned timberland by forest type and species in Colorado's southern Front Range, 1983   30

29. Net annual growth of growing stock on State and privately owned timberland by ownership class and species in Colorado's southern Front Range, 1982   31

30. Net annual growth of sawtimber (International ¼-inch rule) on State and privately owned timberland by ownership class and species in Colorado's southern Front Range, 1982   31

31. Net annual growth of sawtimber (Scribner rule) on State and privately owned timberland by ownership class and species in Colorado's southern Front Range, 1982   32

32. Net annual growth of growing stock on State and privately owned timberland by species and diameter class in Colorado's southern Front Range, 1982 33

33. Net annual growth of sawtimber (International ¼-inch rule) on State and privately owned timberland by species and diameter class in Colorado's southern Front Range, 1982 34

34. Net annual growth of sawtimber (Scribner rule) on State and privately owned timberland by species and diameter class in Colorado's southern Front Range, 1982 35

35. Annual mortality of growing stock on State and privately owned timberland by ownership class and species in Colorado's southern Front Range, 1982 36

36. Annual mortality of sawtimber (International ¼-inch rule) on State and privately owned timberland by ownership class and species in Colorado's southern Front Range, 1982 36

37. Annual mortality of sawtimber (Scribner rule) on State and privately owned timberland by ownership class and species in Colorado's southern Front Range, 1982 37

38. Annual mortality of growing stock on State and privately owned timberland by species and diameter class in Colorado's southern Front Range, 1982 37

39 Annual mortality of sawtimber (International ¼-inch rule) on State and privately owned timberland by species and diameter class in Colorado's southern Front Range, 1982 38

40. Annual mortality of sawtimber (Scribner rule) on State and privately owned timberland by species and diameter class in Colorado's southern Front Range, 1982 38

41. Annual mortality of growing stock on State and privately owned timberland by cause of death and species in Colorado's southern Front Range, 1982 39

42. Annual mortality of sawtimber (International ¼-inch rule) on State and privately owned timberland by cause of death and species in Colorado's southern Front Range, 1982 39

43. Annual mortality of sawtimber (Scribner rule) on State and privately owned timberland by cause of death and species in Colorado's southern Front Range, 1982 40

44. Area of State and privately owned woodland by ownership class and forest type in Colorado's southern Front Range, 1983 40

45. Net volume of State and privately owned woodland by ownership class and species in Colorado's southern Front Range, 1983 41

46. Net annual growth of State and privately owned woodland by ownership class and species in Colorado's southern Front Range, 1982 41

Colorado's Southern Front Range: Forest Statistics for State and Private Land, 1983

Roger C. Conner
William T. Pawley

INTRODUCTION

This resource bulletin reports the findings of the Forest Survey inventory of a sample area defined as State and private lands in Chaffee, Costilla, Custer, Fremont, Huerfano, Las Animas, and Pueblo Counties of the southern Front Range in Colorado (fig. 1). The two-phase survey began with prefield work in June 1981. The field phase involved, in whole or in part, successive summers from 1981 to 1984 with the bulk of the data collected in 1982.

The data in this report pertain only to the State and private forest resources of the counties listed above. Data for lands administered by various public agencies such as

National Forest Systems and Bureau of Land Management will be included in a subsequent, comprehensive statewide report that will include all lands and all owners.

The primary objective of Forest Survey—a continuing, nationwide undertaking of the Forest Service, U.S. Department of Agriculture—is to provide an assessment of the renewable resources for forest and rangelands of the Nation. Fundamental to the accomplishment of the objective are the periodic State-by-State resource inventories. Originally, Forest Survey was authorized by the McSweeney-McNary Act of 1928. The current authorization is through the Renewable Resources Research Act of 1978.

COLORADO

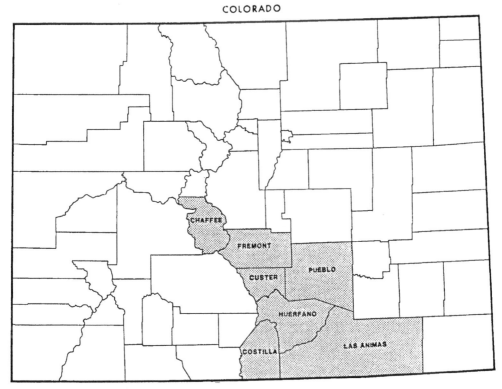

Figure 1—Counties covered by this report.

The Intermountain Research Station with headquarters in Ogden, UT, conducts the forest resource inventories for the Rocky Mountain States of Arizona, Colorado, Idaho, Montana, New Mexico, Nevada, western South Dakota, Utah, Wyoming, western Texas, and Oklahoma's Panhandle. These inventories provide information on the extent and condition of State and privately owned forest lands and most other lands not in the National Forest System, volume of timber, and rates of timber growth, removals, and mortality.

These data, when combined with similar information on National Forest lands, provide a basis for forming forest policies and programs and for the orderly development and use of the resources.

HIGHLIGHTS

Area

- State and private lands comprise nearly 6.9 million acres, or 81 percent of the total land area in Colorado's southern Front Range (fig. 2).
- Forests occupy over 2 million acres, including reserved land, or 30 percent of the total State and private land area.
- About 47 percent of the forest land, 948,500 acres, is classified nonreserved timberland, and 95 percent of this area is privately owned.
- Approximately 1.1 million acres are classified as nonreserved woodland, 92 percent of which is privately owned.
- Ponderosa pine forest type occurs on 50 percent of the privately owned timberland, while Douglas-fir, spruce, and white fir forest types combined make up 29 percent of the area.

- Nearly 94 percent of the woodland area is occupied by juniper or pinyon-juniper forest types, 92 percent of which is privately owned.

Inventory

- Timberland growing-stock volume is about 1.1 billion cubic feet, and sawtimber volume totals 3.2 billion board feet (International ¼-inch rule).
- Of the timberland growing-stock volume, 28 percent, about 290 million cubic feet, is ponderosa pine, with Engelmann spruce (22 percent), Douglas-fir (21 percent), and lodgepole pine (7 percent) adding another 50 percent.
- Woodland volume amounts to about 338 million cubic feet, 97 percent of which is pinyon and juniper species, and woodland hardwoods the remaining 3 percent.
- Private ownership accounts for 96 percent of the timberland growing-stock volume and 92 percent of the woodland volume.
- Nearly 89 percent of the timberland growing-stock volume is in trees less than 19 inches diameter at breast height (d.b.h.).
- About 81 percent of the sawtimber volume, 2.6 billion board feet (International ¼-inch rule), is in trees less than 19 inches d.b.h.
- Rough, rotten, and salvable dead trees total about 65 million cubic feet, about 6 percent of the timberland sound wood volume.
- About a fifth of the timberland area is capable of producing more than 50 cubic feet of wood per acre per year. However, net annual growth in 1982 was just over 21 cubic feet per acre per year.
- Nearly 65 percent of both the timberland growing-stock and sawtimber volumes are in Las Animas and Costilla Counties.

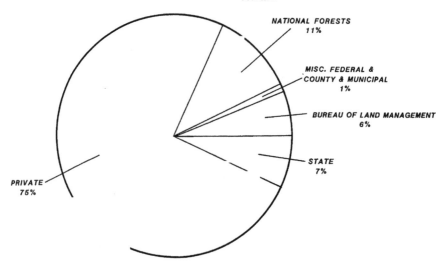

Figure 2—Distribution of land area in Colorado's southern Front Range by owner group.

Components of Change

Growth
- Net annual growth for timberland was over 20.2 million cubic feet in 1982, of which 97 percent was on private land.
- Ponderosa pine and lodgepole pine each account for 25 percent of the timberland net growth, with Engelmann spruce (17 percent) and Douglas-fir (12 percent) adding to the remainder.
- Woodland net annual growth was about 4.6 million cubic feet in 1982, of which 92 percent was on private land.

Mortality
- The annual mortality of 4 million cubic feet of growing stock offsets 17 percent of the timberland gross annual growth.
- Douglas-fir accounts for more than 1 million cubic feet, 26 percent of the timberland annual mortality.
- Weather, insects, and disease caused 68 percent of the mortality.

Removals
- An estimated 1.5 million cubic feet of industrial roundwood material (8.7 million board feet, International ¼-inch rule) was harvested in 1982, of which 56 percent came from State and private land (McLain 1985).
- Custer and Huerfano Counties combined account for 45 percent of the industrial roundwood cubic-foot volume harvested.
- Ponderosa pine contributed the largest percentage to the total board-foot (International ¼-inch rule) harvest (56 percent), with Douglas-fir (23 percent) and spruce (15 percent) accounting for most of the remaining percentage (includes all land owners in the sample area).
- Sawlogs accounted for nearly 100 percent of the industrial roundwood volume harvested (includes all land owners in the sample area).
- Total fuelwood harvest was about 28,500 cords (2.3 million cubic feet) in 1982, of which about 84 percent was cut from State and private land. This was 1.5 times the industrial roundwood harvest (McLain 1985).
- Of the fuelwood, 59 percent was harvested from Pueblo County, and nearly 75 percent of this volume was taken from private land (McLain and Booth 1985).
- Cottonwood accounted for 64 percent of the total fuelwood harvest, with lodgepole pine (20 percent) and pinyon (15 percent) making up most of the remaining percentage (McLain and Booth 1985) (includes all land owners in the sample area).
- Over 99 percent of fuelwood harvested (23,700 cords) from State and private land was from dead trees (McLain and Booth 1985).

HOW THE INVENTORY WAS CONDUCTED

The inventory was designed to provide reliable statistics at the State and sample area levels.

Prefield

Primary area estimates were based on the classification of 34,355 sample points systematically placed on the latest aerial photographs available. The photo points, adjusted to meet known land areas, were used to stratify and compute area expansion factors for the field sample data.

Field

Land classification and estimates for timber characteristics and volume were based on observations or measurements or both recorded at 829 ground sample locations, of which 281 were forested. Sample trees were selected using a 5-point sample cluster, which included 1/300-acre fixed radius plots for trees less than 5 inches d.b.h., and 40 basal area factor variable radius plots for trees 5 inches d.b.h. or larger.

Compilation

All photo and field data were loaded onto tape and stored for computer editing, computation, and tabulation. Final estimates from these data were based on statistical summaries, a portion of which is included in this bulletin. Volume and defect were computed using equations developed by Edminster and others (1980, 1981), Kemp (1958), Chojnacky (1985), Meyers (1964), and Meyers and others (1972).

DATA RELIABILITY

Individual cells within tables should be used with caution. Some are based on small sample sizes resulting in high sampling errors. The standard error percentages shown in tables 1 and 2 were calculated at the 67 percent confidence level.

TERMINOLOGY AND DATA TABLES

The following section contains definitions that are relevant to the timber resource data in this bulletin. Forest area and timber resource data for Colorado's southern Front Range are displayed in tables 3 through 61.

TERMINOLOGY

Acceptable trees—Growing-stock trees meeting specified standards of size and quality, but not qualifying as desirable trees.

Area condition class—A classification of timberland reflecting the degree to which the site is being utilized by growing-stock trees and other conditions affecting current and prospective timber growth (see Stocking):
   Class 10—Areas fully stocked with desirable trees and not overstocked.
   Class 20—Areas fully stocked with desirable trees but overstocked with all live trees.
   Class 30—Areas medium to fully stocked with desirable trees and with less than 30 percent of the area controlled by other trees, or inhibiting vegetation or surface conditions that will prevent occupancy by desirable trees, or both.

Class 40—Areas medium to fully stocked with desirable trees and with 30 percent or more of the area controlled by other trees, or conditions that ordinarily prevent occupancy by desirable trees, or both.

Class 50—Areas poorly stocked with desirable trees but fully stocked with growing-stock trees.

Class 60—Areas poorly stocked with desirable trees but with medium to full stocking of growing-stock trees.

Class 70—Areas nonstocked or poorly stocked with desirable trees and poorly stocked with growing-stock trees.

Class 80—Low-risk old-growth stands.

Class 90—High-risk old-growth stands.

Nonstocked—Areas less than 10 percent stocked with growing-stock trees.

Basal area—The cross-sectional area of a tree expressed in square feet. For timber species the calculation is based on diameter at breast height (d.b.h.); for woodland species it is based on diameter at root collar (d.r.c.).

Cord—A pile of stacked wood equivalent to 128 cubic feet of wood and air space having standard dimensions of 4 by 4 by 8 feet.

Cull trees—Live trees that are unmerchantable now or prospectively (see Rough trees and Rotten trees).

Cull volume—Portions of a tree's volume that are not usable for wood products because of rot, form, missing material, or other cubic-foot defect. Form and sound defects include severe sweep and crook, forks, extreme form reduction, large deformities, and dead material.

Deferred forest land—Forest lands within the National Forest System that are under study for possible inclusion in the Wilderness System.

Desirable trees—Growing-stock trees (1) having no serious defect in quality to limit present or prospective use for timber products, (2) of relatively high vigor, and (3) containing no pathogens that may result in death or serious deterioration within the next decade.

Diameter at breast height (d.b.h.)—Diameter of the stem measured at 4.5 feet above the ground.

Diameter at root collar (d.r.c.)—Diameter equivalent at the point nearest the ground line that represents the basal area of the tree stem or stems.

Diameter classes—Tree diameters, either d.b.h. or d.r.c., grouped into 2-inch classes labeled by the midpoint of the class.

Farmer-owned lands—Lands owned by a person who operates a farm and who either does the work or directly supervises the work.

Forest industry lands—Lands owned by companies or individuals operating a primary wood-processing plant.

Forest land—Land at least 10 percent stocked by forest trees of any size, including land that formerly had such tree cover and that will be naturally or artificially regenerated. The minimum area for classification of forest land is 1 acre. Roadside, streamside, and shelterbelt strips of timber must have a crown width at least 120 feet wide to qualify as forest land. Unimproved roads and trails, streams, and clearings in forest areas are classified as forest if less than 120 feet wide.

Forest trees—Woody plants having a well-developed stem or stems, usually more than 12 feet in height at maturity, with a generally well-defined crown.

Forest type—A classification of forest land based upon and named for the tree species presently forming a plurality of live-tree stocking.

Growing-stock trees—Live sawtimber trees, poletimber trees, saplings, and seedlings of timber species meeting specified standards of quality and vigor; excludes cull trees.

Growing-stock volume—Net cubic-foot volume in live growing-stock trees from a 1-foot stump to a minimum 4-inch top (of central stem) outside bark or to the point where the central stem breaks into limbs.

Growth—See definition for Net annual growth.

Hardwood trees—Dicotyledonous trees, usually broad-leaved and deciduous.

High-risk old-growth stands—Timber stands over 100 years old in which the majority of the trees are not expected to survive more than 10 years.

Indian lands—Indian lands held in trust by the Federal Government.

Industrial wood—All commercial roundwood products except fuelwood.

Land area—The area of dry land and land temporarily or partially covered by water such as marshes, swamps, and river flood plains, streams, sloughs, estuaries, and canals less than 120 feet wide; and lakes, reservoirs, and ponds less than 1 acre in size.

Logging residues—The unused portions of growing-stock trees cut or killed by logging.

Low-risk old-growth stands—Timber stands over 100 years old in which the majority of the trees are expected to survive more than 10 years.

Miscellaneous Federal lands—Lands administered by Federal agencies other than the Forest Service, U.S. Department of Agriculture, or Bureau of Land Management, U.S. Department of the Interior.

Mortality—The net volume of growing-stock trees that have died from natural causes during a specified period.

National Forest lands—Public lands administered by the Forest Service, U.S. Department of Agriculture.

National Resource lands—Public lands administered by the Bureau of Land Management, U.S. Department of the Interior.

Net annual growth—The net average annual increase in the volume of trees during a specified period.

Net volume in board feet—The gross board-foot volume in the sawlog portion of growing-stock trees, less deductions for cull volume.

Net volume in cubic feet—Gross cubic-foot volume in the merchantable portion of trees less deductions for cull volume. For timber species, volume is computed for the merchantable stem from a 1-foot stump to a minimum 4-inch top diameter outside bark, or to the point where the central stem breaks into limbs. For woodland species, volume is computed outside bark (o.b.) for all woody material above d.r.c. that is larger than 1.5 inches in diameter (o.b.).

Nonforest land—Land that does not currently qualify as forest land.

Nonindustrial private—All private ownerships except forest industry.

Nonstocked areas—Forest land less than 10 percent stocked with live trees.

Old-growth stands—Stands of timber species over 100 years old.

Other private land—Privately owned land other than forest industry or farmer-owned.

Other public land—Public land administered by agencies other than the Forest Service, U.S. Department of Agriculture.

Other removals—The net volume of growing-stock trees removed from the inventory by cultural operations such as timber-stand improvement, by land clearing, and by changes in land use such as a shift to wilderness.

Poletimber stands—Stands at least 10 percent stocked with growing-stock trees, in which half or more of the stocking is sawtimber or poletimber trees or both, with poletimber stocking exceeding that of sawtimber (see definition for Stocking).

Poletimber trees—Live trees of timber species at least 5 inches d.b.h. but smaller than sawtimber size.

Potential growth—The average net annual cubic-foot growth per acre at culmination of mean annual growth attainable in fully stocked natural stands.

Primary wood-processing plants—Plants using roundwood products such as sawlogs, pulpwood bolts, veneer logs, etc.

Productivity class—A classification of forest land in terms of potential growth.

Removals—The net volume of growing-stock trees removed from the inventory by harvesting, cultural operations, land clearings, or changes in land use.

Reserved forest land—Forest land withdrawn from tree utilization through statute or administrative designation.

Residues:
Coarse residues—Plant residues suitable for chipping, such as slabs, edgings, and ends.
Fine residues—Plant residues not suitable for chipping, such as sawdust, shavings, and veneer clippings.
Plant residues—Wood materials from primary manufacturing plants that are not used for any product.

Rotten tree—A live poletimber or sawtimber tree with more than 67 percent of its total volume cull (cubic-foot) and with more than half of the cull volume attributable to rotten or missing material.

Rough tree—A live poletimber or sawtimber tree with more than 67 percent of its total volume cull (cubic-foot) and with less than half of the cull volume attributable to rotten or missing material.

Roundwood—Logs, bolts, or other round sections cut from trees.

Salvable dead trees—Standing or down dead trees that are currently merchantable by regional standards.

Saplings—Live trees of timber species 1 to 4.9 inches d.b.h., or woodland species 1 to 2.9 inches d.r.c.

Sapling and seedling stands—Timberland stands at least 10 percent stocked on which more than half of the stocking is saplings or seedlings or both.

Sawlog portion—That part of the bole of sawtimber trees between a 1-foot stump and the sawlog top.

Sawlog top—The point on the bole of sawtimber trees above which a sawlog cannot be produced. The minimum sawlog top is 7 inches diameter o.b. for softwoods, and 9 inches diameter o.b. for hardwoods.

Sawtimber stands—Stands at least 10 percent stocked with growing-stock trees, with half or more of total stocking in sawtimber or poletimber trees, and with sawtimber stocking at least equal to poletimber stocking.

Sawtimber trees—Live trees of timber species meeting regional size and defect specifications. Softwood trees must be at least 9 inches d.b.h. and hardwood trees 11 inches d.b.h.

Sawtimber volume—Net volume in board feet of the sawlog portion of live sawtimber trees.

Seedlings—Established live trees of timber species less than 1 inch d.b.h. or woodland species less than 1 inch d.r.c.

Softwood trees—Monocotyledonous trees, usually evergreen, having needle or scalelike leaves.

Standard error—An expression of the degree of confidence that can be placed on an estimated total or average obtained by statistical sampling methods. Standard errors do not include technique errors that could occur in photo classification of areas, field measurements, or compilation of data.

Stand-size classes—A classification of forest land based on the predominant size of trees present (see Sawtimber stands, Poletimber stands, and Sapling and seedling stands).

State, county, and municipal lands—Lands administered by States, counties, or local public agencies, or lands leased by these governmental units for more than 50 years.

Stocking—An expression of the extent to which growing space is effectively utilized by present or potential growing-stock trees of timber species. Percentage stocking is the ratio of actual stocking to full stocking for comparable sites and stands, using basal area as the basis for comparison.

Timberland—Forest land where timber species make up at least 10 percent stocking.

Timber species—Tree species traditionally used for industrial wood products. In the Rocky Mountain States, these include aspen and cottonwood hardwood species and all softwood species except pinyon and juniper.

Timber stand improvement—Treatments such as thinning, pruning, release cutting, girdling, weeding, or poisoning of unwanted trees aimed at improving growing conditions for the remaining trees.

5

Upper-stem portion—That part of the main stem or fork of sawtimber trees above the sawlog top to a minimum top diameter of 4 inches o.b. or to the point where the main stem or fork breaks into limbs.

Water—Streams, sloughs, estuaries, and canals more than 120 feet wide, and lakes, reservoirs, and ponds more than 1 acre in size at mean high water level.

Wilderness—An area of undeveloped land currently included in the Wilderness System, managed so as to preserve its natural conditions and retain its primeval character and influence.

Woodland—Forest land where timber species make up less than 10 percent stocking.

Woodland species dead volume—Net volume of dead woodland trees and dead net volume portion of live woodland tree species.

Woodland species live volume—Net cubic-foot volume in live woodland tree species.

Woodland species—Tree species not usually converted into industrial wood products. Common uses are fuelwood, fenceposts, and Christmas trees.

REFERENCES

Chojnacky, David C. 1985. Pinyon-juniper volume equations for the central Rocky Mountain States. Res. Pap. INT-339. Ogden, UT: U.S. Department of Agriculture, Forest Service, Intermountain Forest and Range Experiment Station. 27 p.

Edminster, Carleton B.; Beeson, Robert T.; Metcalf, Gary E. 1980. Volume tables and point-sampling factors for ponderosa pine in the Front Range of Colorado. Res. Pap. RM-218. Fort Collins, CO: U.S. Department of Agriculture, Forest Service, Rocky Mountain Forest and Range Experiment Station. 14 p.

Edminster, Carleton B.; Mowrer, H. Todd; Hinds, Thomas E. 1981. Volume tables and point-sampling factors for aspen in Colorado. Res. Pap. RM-232. Fort Collins, CO: U.S. Department of Agriculture, Forest Service, Rocky Mountain Forest and Range Experiment Station. 16 p.

Kemp, Paul D. 1958. Volume tables. Unpublished report on file at: U.S. Department of Agriculture, Forest Service, Intermountain Research Station, Ogden, UT.

McLain, William H. 1985. Colorado's industrial roundwood production and mill residues, 1982. Resour. Bull. INT-35. Ogden, UT: U.S. Department of Agriculture, Forest Service, Intermountain Research Station. 13 p.

McLain, William H.; Booth, Gordon D. 1985. Colorado's 1982 fuelwood harvest. Resour. Bull. INT-36. Ogden, UT: U.S. Department of Agriculture, Forest Service, Intermountain Research Station. 11 p.

Meyers, Clifford A. 1964. Volume tables and point-sampling factors for lodgepole pine in Colorado and Wyoming. Res. Pap. RM-6. Fort Collins, CO: U.S. Department of Agriculture, Forest Service, Rocky Mountain Forest and Range Experiment Station. 16 p.

Meyers, Clifford A.; Edminster, Carleton B. 1972. Volume tables and point-sampling factors for Engelmann spruce in Colorado and Wyoming. Res. Pap. RM-95. Fort Collins, CO: U.S. Department of Agriculture, Forest Service, Rocky Mountain Forest and Range Experiment Station. 23 p.

FOREST SURVEY TABLES

Table 1.-- Area of State and privately owned forest land with percent standard error in Colorado's southern
Front Range, 1983

Item	Softwoods		Hardwoods		All types	
	Acres	Percent standard error	Acres	Percent standard error	Acres	Percent standard error
Timberland	848,838	±6.4	99,624	±23.5	948,462	±5.6
Woodland	1,003,191	±6.3	69,126	±40.7	1,072,317	±6.3
Reserved forest land:[1]						
Timberland	--		500		500	
Woodland	2,900		31		2,931	
Total forest land	1,854,929		169,281		2,024,210	

[1]Reserved land areas are estimated from aerial photos without field verification; therefore, standard
errors are not calculated.

Table 2.--Net volume, net annual growth, and annual mortality of growing stock and sawtimber on State and
privately owned timberland with percent standard error in Colorado's southern Front Range

Item	Softwoods		Hardwoods		All species	
	Volume	Percent standard error	Volume	Percent standard error	Volume	Percent standard error
Net volume, 1983:						
Growing stock (M cubic feet)	958,829	± 9.9	97,606	±23.5	1,056,435	± 9.1
Sawtimber[1] (M board feet)	3,098,649	±12.1	119,581	±30.6	3,218,230	±11.7
Sawtimber[2] (M board feet)	2,618,818	±12.1	102,426	±30.8	2,721,244	±11.7
Net annual growth, 1982:						
Growing stock (M cubic feet)	17,828	±16.8	2,390	±37.7	20,218	±15.3
Sawtimber[1] (M board feet)	60,237	±19.7	10,226	±64.4	70,463	±18.3
Sawtimber[2] (M board feet)	50,080	±19.7	8,828	±64.3	58,908	±18.5
Annual mortality, 1982:						
Growing stock (M cubic feet)	3,408	±29.5	594	±75.7	4,002	±27.7
Sawtimber[1] (M board feet)	11,624	±33.8	1,463	±70.0	13,087	±32.1
Sawtimber[2] (M board feet)	10,010	±33.5	1,257	±70.0	11,267	±31.9

[1]International ¼-inch rule.

[2]Scribner rule.

Table 3.--Total land and water area by ownership class in Colorado's southern Front Range, 1983

Ownership class	Area
	- - Acres - -
Land:	
Public:	
National Forest	964,032
Other:	
Bureau of Land Management	531,364
Miscellaneous federal	79,085
State	533,360
County and municipal	49,113
Total other public	1,192,922
Total public	2,156,954
Private	6,319,058
Total land area	8,476,012
Census water	27,046
Total land and water[1]	8,503,058

[1]U.S. Bureau of the Census, land and water area of the United States, 1980.

Table 4.--Total land area on State and privately owned land by major land class and ownership class in Colorado's southern Front Range, 1983

Land class	Ownership class		
	State	Nonindustrial private	Total
	- - - - - - - - - - - Acres - - - - - - - - - - -		
Timberland:			
Reserved	500	--	500
Nonreserved	42,811	905,651	948,462
Total	43,311	905,651	948,962
Woodland:			
Reserved	2,931	--	2,931
Nonreserved	80,755	991,562	1,072,317
Total	83,686	991,562	1,075,248
Total forest land:			
Reserved	3,431	--	3,431
Nonreserved	123,566	1,897,213	2,020,779
Total	126,997	1,897,213	2,024,210
Nonforest land	406,363	4,421,845	4,828,208
Total land area	533,360	6,319,058	6,852,418

Table 5.--Area of forest land on State and privately owned land by forest type, ownership class, and land class in Colorado's southern Front Range, 1983

| | Ownership class and land class | | | | | | |
| Forest type | State | | Nonindustrial private | | All owners | | |
	Reserved	Nonreserved	Reserved	Nonreserved	Reserved	Nonreserved	Total
			- - - - - - - - - - - - - - - - - Acres -				
Douglas-fir	--	6,653	--	119,531	--	126,184	126,184
Ponderosa pine	--	24,561	--	446,341	--	470,902	470,902
Lodgepole pine		884	--	36,273	--	37,157	37,157
Limber pine		458	--	19,009	--	19,467	19,467
Spruce subalpine-fir	--	1,381	--	43,536	--	44,917	44,917
White fir	--	3,011	--	64,589	--	67,600	67,600
Spruce	--	2,340	--	80,271	--	82,611	82,611
Aspen	--	2,694	--	66,831	--	69,525	69,525
Cottonwood	500	829	--	29,270	500	30,099	30,599
Total timberland	500	42,811	--	905,651	500	948,462	948,962
Pinyon-juniper	2,900	60,471	--	733,108	2,900	793,579	796,479
Juniper	--	18,231	--	191,381	--	209,612	209,612
Oak	31	1,824	--	57,569	31	59,393	59,424
Other west hardwoods	--	229	--	9,504	--	9,733	9,733
Total woodland	2,931	80,755	--	991,562	2,931	1,072,317	1,075,248
Total all types	3,431	123,566	--	1,897,213	3,431	2,020,779	2,024,210

Table 6.--Cubic feet of net volume in trees on State and privately owned
forest land by species and ownership class in Colorado's southern
Front Range, 1983

Species	Ownership class		
	State	Nonindustrial private	Total
	- - - - - - - Thousand cubic feet - - - - - - -		
Douglas-fir	9,634	208,946	218,580
Ponderosa pine	13,560	276,887	290,447
Lodgepole pine	1,345	69,670	71,015
Whitebark pine	598	19,044	19,642
Limber pine	816	21,682	22,498
Subalpine fir	1,474	46,062	47,536
White fir	2,865	56,999	59,864
Engelmann spruce	6,481	222,886	229,367
Aspen	2,347	74,192	76,539
Cottonwood	285	20,782	21,067
Total timberland species	39,405	1,017,150	1,056,555
Pinyon/juniper	28,240	333,617	361,857
Woodland hardwoods	1,308	24,367	25,675
Total woodland species	29,548	357,984	387,532
Total all species	68,953	1,375,134	1,444,087

Table 7.--Cubic feet of net annual growth in trees on State and privately owned
forest land by species and ownership class in Colorado's southern
Front Range, 1982

Species	Ownership class		
	State	Nonindustrial private	Total
	- - - - - - Thousand cubic feet - - - - - - -		
Douglas-fir	139	2,214	2,353
Ponderosa pine	250	4,762	5,012
Lodgepole pine	97	4,879	4,976
Whitebark pine	7	224	231
Limber pine	11	235 ·	246
Subalpine fir	37	1,107	1,144
White fir	-20	374	354
Engelmann spruce	122	3,392	3,514
Aspen	63	1,572	1,635
Cottonwood	3	752	755
Total timberland species	709	19,511	20,220
Pinyon/juniper	391	4,376 ·	4,767
Woodland hardwoods	-4	160	156
Total woodland species	387	4,536	4,923
Total all species	1,096	24,047	25,143

Table 8.--Cubic feet of annual mortality in trees on State and privately owned
forest land by species and ownership class in Colorado's southern
Front Range, 1982

Species	Ownership class		
	State	Nonindustrial private	Total
	- - - - - - - Thousand cubic feet - - - - - - -		
Douglas-fir	43	1,000	1,043
Ponderosa pine	25	622	647
Lodgepole pine	--	--	--
Whitebark pine		--	
Limber pine	--	--	--
Subalpine fir	--	--	--
White fir	78	913	991
Engelmann spruce	--	727	727
Aspen	--	594	594
Cottonwood	--	--	--
Total timberland species	146	3,856	4,002
Pinyon/juniper	18	476	494
Woodland hardwoods	34	342	376
Total woodland species	52	818	870
Total all species	198	4,674	4,872

Table 9.--Area of State and privately owned timberland by forest type, stand-
size class, and productivity class in Colorado's southern Front
Range, 1983

Forest type and stand-size class	Productivity class				Total acres
	85-119	50-84	20-49	0-19	
- - - - - - - - - - - Acres - - - - - - - - - - -					
Douglas-fir:					
Sawtimber	--	14,448	58,930	--	·73,378
Poletimber	--	3,799	45,168	--	48,967
Sapling and seedling	--	--	--	--	--
Nonstocked	--	3,839	--	--	3,839
Total	--	22,086	104,098	--	126,184
Ponderosa pine:					
Sawtimber	--	16,526	254,196	--	270,722
Poletimber	--	12,098	96,418	--	108,516
Sapling and seedling	--	--	--	--	--
Nonstocked	--	--	91,664	--	91,664
Total	--	28,624	442,278	--	470,902
Lodgepole pine:					
Sawtimber		--	12,976	--	12,976
Poletimber		--	24,181	--	24,181
Sapling and seedling	--	--	--	--	--
Nonstocked	--	--	--	--	--
Total	--	--	37,157	--	37,157
Limber pine:					
Sawtimber		--	9,733	9,734	19,467
Poletimber			--	--	--
Sapling and seedling	--	--	--	--	--
Nonstocked	--	--	--	--	--
Total	--	--	9,733	9,734	19,467
Spruce-subalpine fir:					
Sawtimber	--	8,263	36,654	--	44,917
Poletimber		--	--		--
Sapling and seedling	--	--	--	--	--
Nonstocked	--	--	--	--	--
Total	--	8,263	36,654	--	44,917

(con.)

Table 9. (con.)

Forest type and stand-size class	Productivity class				Total acres
	85-119	50-84	20-49	0-19	

- - - - - - - - - - - Acres - - - - - - - - - - - - -

White fir:
Sawtimber	--	13,568	28,625	--	42,193
Poletimber	--	8,553	--	--	8,553
Sapling and seedling	--	9,184	3,835	--	13,019
Nonstocked	3,835	--	--	--	3,835
Total	3,835	31,305	32,460	--	67,600

Spruce:
Sawtimber	--	51,101	18,283	--	69,384
Poletimber	4,714	--	3,799	--	8,513
Sapling and seedling	--	--	4,714	--	4,714
Nonstocked	--	--	--	--	--
Total	4,714	51,101	26,796	--	82,611

Aspen:
Sawtimber	--	8,262	9,428	--	17,690
Poletimber	--	14,545	--	--	14,545
Sapling and seedling	--	3,840	10,184	23,266	37,290
Nonstocked	--	--	--	--	--
Total	--	26,647	19,612	23,266	69,525

Cottonwood:
Sawtimber	--	9,957	10,184	--	20,141
Poletimber	--	9,958	--	--	9,958
Sapling and seedling	--	--	--	--	--
Nonstocked	--	--	--	--	--
Total	--	19,915	10,184	--	30,099

All types:
Sawtimber	--	122,125	439,009	9,734	570,868
Poletimber	4,714	48,953	169,566	--	223,233
Sapling and seedling	--	13,024	18,733	23,266	55,023
Nonstocked	3,835	3,839	91,664	--	99,338
Total	8,549	187,941	718,972	33,000	948,462

Table 10.--Area of State owned timberland by forest type, stand-size class, and productivity class in Colorado's southern Front Range, 1983

Forest type and stand-size class	Productivity class				Total acres
	85-119	50-84	20-49	0-19	
	- - - - - - - - - - - - Acres - - - - - - - - - - - -				
Douglas-fir:					
Sawtimber		229	4,157		4,386
Poletimber		656	1,611		2,267
Sapling and seedling	--	--	--	--	--
Nonstocked	--	--	--	--	--
Total	--	885	5,768	--	6,653
Ponderosa pine:					
Sawtimber		853	12,374	--	13,227
Poletimber		698	3,770	--	4,468
Sapling and seedling	--	--	--	--	--
Nonstocked	--	--	6,866	--	6,866
Total	--	1,551	23,010	--	24,561
Lodgepole pine:					
Sawtimber			426	--	426
Poletimber			458	--	458
Sapling and seedling	--	--	--	--	--
Nonstocked	--	--	--	--	--
Total	--	--	884	--	884
Limber pine:					
Sawtimber			229	229	458
Poletimber			--	--	--
Sapling and seedling	--	--	--	--	--
Nonstocked	--	--	--	--	--
Total	--	--	229	229	458
Spruce-subalpine fir:					
Sawtimber		426	955	--	1,381
Poletimber	--	--	--		--
Sapling and seedling	--	--	--	--	--
Nonstocked	--	--	--	--	--
Total	--	426	955	--	1,381

(con.)

Table 10. (con.)

Forest type and stand-size class	Productivity class				Total acres
	85-119	50-84	20-49	0-19	
- - - - - - - - - - Acres - - - - - - - - - - - - -					
White fir:					
Sawtimber		500	1,551		2,051
Poletimber	--	--	--		--
Sapling and seedling	--	418	271	--	689
Nonstocked	271	--	--	--	271
Total	271	918	1,822	--	3,011
Spruce:					
Sawtimber	--	1,183	501	--	1,684
Poletimber		--	656	--	656
Sapling and seedling	--	--	--	--	--
Nonstocked	--	--	--	--	--
Total	--	1,183	1,157	--	2,340
Aspen:					
Sawtimber		426	--	--	426
Poletimber		325	--	--	325
Sapling and seedling	--	--	829	1,114	1,943
Nonstocked	--	--	--	--	--
Total	--	751	829	1,114	2,694
Cottonwood:					
Sawtimber			829	--	829
Poletimber			--		--
Sapling and seedling	--	--	--	--	--
Nonstocked	--	--	--	--	--
Total	--	--	829	--	829
All types:					
Sawtimber	--	3,617	21,022	229	24,868
Poletimber	--	1,679	6,495	--	8,174
Sapling and seedling	--	418	1,100	1,114	2,632
Nonstocked	271	--	6,866	--	7,137
Total	271	5,714	35,483	1,343	42,811

15

Table 11.--Area of nonindustrial privately owned timberland by forest type, stand-size class, and productivity class in Colorado's southern Front Range, 1983

Forest type and stand-size class	Productivity class				Total acres
	85-119	50-84	20-49	0-19	
- - - - - - - - - - Acres - - - - - - - - - - - - -					
Douglas-fir:					
Sawtimber	--	14,219	54,773	--	68,992
Poletimber	--	3,143	43,557	--	46,700
Sapling and seedling	--	--	--	--	--
Nonstocked	--	3,839	--	--	3,839
Total	--	21,201	98,330	--	119,531
Ponderosa pine:					
Sawtimber	--	15,673	241,822	--	257,495
Poletimber	--	11,400	92,648	--	104,048
Sapling and seedling	--	--	--	--	--
Nonstocked	--	--	84,798	--	84,798
Total	--	27,073	419,268	--	446,341
Lodgepole pine:					
Sawtimber		--	12,550	--	12,550
Poletimber		--	23,723	--	23,723
Sapling and seedling	--	--	--	--	--
Nonstocked	--	--	--	--	--
Total	--	--	36,273	--	36,273
Limber pine:					
Sawtimber		--	9,504	9,505	19,009
Poletimber			--	--	--
Sapling and seedling	--	--	--	--	--
Nonstocked	--	--	--	--	--
Total	--	--	9,504	9,505	19,009
Spruce-subalpine fir:					
Sawtimber	--	7,837	35,699	--	43,536
Poletimber		--	--		--
Sapling and seedling	--	--	--	--	--
Nonstocked	--	--	--	--	--
Total	--	7,837	35,699	--	43,536

(con.)

Table 11. (con.)

Forest type and stand-size class	Productivity class				Total acres
	85-119	50-84	20-49	0-19	
- - - - - - - - - - Acres - - - - - - - - - - - - -					
White fir:					
Sawtimber	--	13,068	27,074	--	40,142
Poletimber	--	8,553	--	--	8,553
Sapling and seedling	--	8,766	3,564	--	12,330
Nonstocked	3,564	--	--	--	3,564
Total	3,564	30,387	30,638	--	64,589
Spruce:					
Sawtimber	--	49,918	17,782	--	67,700
Poletimber	4,714	--	3,143	--	7,857
Sapling and seedling	--	--	4,714	--	4,714
Nonstocked	--	--	--	--	--
Total	4,714	49,918	25,639	--	80,271
Aspen:					
Sawtimber	--	7,836	9,428	--	17,264
Poletimber	--	14,220	--	--	14,220
Sapling and seedling	--	3,840	9,355	22,152	35,347
Nonstocked	--	--	--	--	--
Total	--	25,896	18,783	22,152	66,831
Cottonwood:					
Sawtimber	--	9,957	9,355	--	19,312
Poletimber	--	9,958	--	--	9,958
Sapling and seedling	--	--	--	--	--
Nonstocked	--	--	--	--	--
Total	--	19,915	9,355	--	29,270
All types:					
Sawtimber	--	118,508	417,987	9,505	546,000
Poletimber	4,714	47,274	163,071	--	215,059
Sapling and seedling	--	12,606	17,633	22,152	52,391
Nonstocked	3,564	3,839	84,798	--	92,201
Total	8,278	182,227	683,489	31,657	905,651

Table 12.--Area of State and privately owned timberland by stand volume and
ownership class in Colorado's southern Front Range, 1983

Stand volume per acre[1]	Ownership class		
	State	Nonindustrial private	Total
	- - - - - - - - - - Acres - - - - - - - - - -		
Less than 1,500 board feet	19,183	354,655	373,838
1,500 to 4,999 board feet	14,820	319,493	334,313
5,000 to 9,999 board feet	7,310	165,107	172,417
10,000 board feet or more	1,498	66,396	67,894
All classes	42,811	905,651	948,462

[1]International ¼-inch rule.

Table 13.--Area of State and privately owned timberland by forest type and area condition class in Colorado's southern Front Range, 1983

Forest type	Area condition class										
	10	20	30	40	50	60	70	80	90	Nonstocked	All classes
	- Acres -										
Douglas-fir	--	--	--	3,800	39,743	45,837	3,800	3,800	25,365	3,839	126,184
Ponderosa pine	--	--	--	--	33,052	150,189	169,154	--	26,843	91,664	470,902
Lodgepole pine	--	--	--	--	37,157	--	--	--	--	--	37,157
Limber pine	--	--	--	--	--	--	9,733	--	9,734	--	19,467
Spruce-subalpine fir	--	--	--	--	27,226	--	--	4,714	12,977	--	44,917
White fir	--	--	--	--	--	17,691	33,976	--	12,098	3,835	67,600
Spruce	--	27,226	--	--	9,733	27,675	14,898	--	17,977	--	82,611
Aspen	--	--	--	--	44,894	9,733	14,898	--	--	--	69,525
Cottonwood	--	--	--	--	--	9,958	10,184	--	9,957	--	30,099
All types	--	27,226	--	3,800	191,805	261,083	241,745	8,514	114,951	99,338	948,462

Table 14.--Number of growing-stock trees on State and privately owned timberland by species and diameter class in Colorado's southern Front Range, 1983

Species	Diameter class (inches at breast height)															All classes
	1.0-2.9	3.0-4.9	5.0-6.9	7.0-8.9	9.0-10.9	11.0-12.9	13.0-14.9	15.0-16.9	17.0-18.9	19.0-20.9	21.0-22.9	23.0-24.9	25.0-26.9	27.0-28.9	29.0+	
	- Thousand trees -															
Douglas-fir	1,040	9,416	7,590	7,022	2,368	1,547	1,501	1,266	495	255	245	79	49	9	18	32,900
Ponderosa pine	3,202	15,071	15,417	13,763	6,770	2,985	2,447	840	921	331	118	37	73	18	29	62,022
Lodgepole pine	1,445	9,583	13,995	3,144	779	333	184	--	--	--	--	--	--	--	--	29,463
Whitebark pine	--	--	864	760	351	282	227	154	46	17	11	--	--	--	--	2,701
Limber pine	--	3,467	1,099	170	274	517	103	54	48	74	--	--	10	18	8	5,853
Subalpine fir	2,065	3,933	4,503	2,886	1,385	143	--	22	23	--	--	--	--	--	--	14,960
White fir	7,266	3,460	6,173	2,578	1,363	789	229	261	59	70	64	--	--	16	6	22,334
Engelmann spruce	18,300	8,089	5,013	6,126	2,934	3,566	1,440	871	529	176	70	25	58	--	--	47,197
Total softwoods	33,318	53,019	54,654	36,449	16,224	10,162	6,131	3,468	2,121	923	508	141	190	61	61	217,430
Aspen	33,419	19,627	13,641	4,371	1,391	587	214	102	--	--	--	--	--	--	--	73,352
Cottonwood	--	--	1,435	685	884	107	--	59	45	--	--	--	--	--	63	3,278
Total hardwoods	33,419	19,627	15,076	5,056	2,275	694	214	161	45	--	--	--	--	--	63	76,630
All species	66,737	72,646	69,730	41,505	18,499	10,856	6,345	3,629	2,166	923	508	141	190	61	124	294,060

Table 15.--Number of cull and salvable dead trees on State and privately owned timberland by ownership class, and softwoods and hardwoods in Colorado's southern Front Range, 1983

Ownership class and species group	Cull trees			Salvable dead trees	All dead trees
	Sound	Rotten	Total		
	- - - - - - - - - Thousand trees - - - - - - - - -				
State:					
Softwoods	62	47	109	459	568
Hardwoods	--	17	17	171	188
Total	62	64	126	630	756
Nonindustrial private:					
Softwoods	1,134	1,040	2,174	9,194	11,368
Hardwoods	--	590	590	4,137	4,727
Total	1,134	1,630	2,764	13,331	16,095
Total:					
Softwoods	1,196	1,087	2,283	9,653	11,936
Hardwoods	--	607	607	4,308	4,915
Total	1,196	1,694	2,890	13,961	16,851

Table 16.--Net volume of growing stock on State and privately owned timberland by ownership class, forest type, and stand-size class in Colorado's southern Front Range, 1983

- - - - - - - - - - Thousand cubic feet - - - - - - - - - - -

State:					
	Douglas-fir	7,010	3,336	--	--	10,346
	Ponderosa pine	9,895	3,449	--	483	13,827
	Lodgepole pine	602	736	--	--	1,338
	Limber pine	387	--	--	--	387
	Spruce-subalpine fir	3,340	--	--		3,340
	White fir	2,217	--	218		2,435
	Spruce	4,541	892	--		5,433
	Aspen	823	735	345	--	1,903
	Cottonwood	387	--	--	--	387
	All types	29,202	9,148	563	483	39,396
Nonindustrial private:					
	Douglas-fir	136,903	64,855	--	386	202,144
	Ponderosa pine	203,776	77,344	--	6,736	287,856
	Lodgepole pine	29,466	44,876	--	--	74,342
	Limber pine	16,073	--	--	--	16,073
	Spruce-subalpine fir	103,542	--	--		103,542
	White fir	43,914	13,027	5,269	--	62,210
	Spruce	178,484	9,144	750		188,378
	Aspen	25,130	30,047	5,378	--	60,555
	Cottonwood	8,708	13,231	--	--	21,939
	All types	745,996	252,524	11,397	7,122	1,017,039
Total:					
	Douglas-fir	143,913	68,191	--	386	212,490
	Ponderosa pine	213,671	80,793	--	7,219	301,683
	Lodgepole pine	30,068	45,612	--	--	75,680
	Limber pine	16,460	--	--	--	16,460
	Spruce-subalpine fir	106,882	--	--		106,882
	White fir	46,131	13,027	5,487		64,645
	Spruce	183,025	10,036	750		193,811
	Aspen	25,953	30,782	5,723	--	62,458
	Cottonwood	9,095	13,231	--	--	22,326
	All types	775,198	261,672	11,960	7,605	1,056,435

Table 17.--Net volume of sawtimber (International ¼-inch rule) on State and privately owned timberland by ownership class, forest type, and stand-size class in Colorado's southern Front Range, 1983

Ownership class	Forest type	Stand-size class				
		Sawtimber	Poletimber	Sapling/ seedling	Nonstocked	All classes
		- - - - - Thousand board feet, International ¼-inch rule - - - -				
State:						
	Douglas-fir	23,715	8,699	--	--	32,414
	Ponderosa pine	36,415	5,879	--	2,215	44,509
	Lodgepole pine	1,503	131	--	--	1,634
	Limber pine	1,183	--	--	--	1,183
	Spruce-subalpine fir	10,127	--	--		10,127
	White fir	8,113	--	902		9,015
	Spruce	17,693	648	--		18,341
	Aspen	2,334	992	371	--	3,697
	Cottonwood	1,811	--	--	--	1,811
	All types	102,894	16,349	1,273	2,215	122,731
Nonindustrial private:						
	Douglas-fir	505,199	165,425	--	1,270	671,894
	Ponderosa pine	724,110	127,445	--	31,914	883,469
	Lodgepole pine	79,350	5,417	--	--	84,767
	Limber pine	49,126	--	--	--	49,126
	Spruce-subalpine fir	325,685	--	--		325,685
	White fir	151,226	17,720	19,031		187,977
	Spruce	696,720	9,476	2,052		708,248
	Aspen	77,614	47,485	11,633	--	136,732
	Cottonwood	40,730	6,871	--	--	47,601
	All types	2,649,760	379,839	32,716	33,184	3,095,499
Total:						
	Douglas-fir	528,914	174,124	--	1,270	704,308
	Ponderosa pine	760,525	133,324	--	34,129	927,978
	Lodgepole pine	80,853	5,548	--	--	86,401
	Limber pine	50,309	--	--	--	50,309
	Spruce-subalpine fir	335,812	--	--		335,812
	White fir	159,339	17,720	19,933		196,992
	Spruce	714,413	10,124	2,052		726,589
	Aspen	79,948	48,477	12,004	--	140,429
	Cottonwood	42,541	6,871	--	--	49,412
	All types	2,752,654	396,188	33,989	35,399	3,218,230

Table 18.--Net volume of sawtimber (Scribner rule) on State and privately owned timberland by ownership class, forest type, and stand-size class in Colorado's southern Front Range, 1983

Ownership class	Forest type	Stand-size class				All classes
		Sawtimber	Poletimber	Sapling/ seedling	Nonstocked	
		- - - - - - - Thousand board feet, Scribner rule - - - - - - -				
State:						
	Douglas-fir	20,040	7,343	--	--	27,383
	Ponderosa pine	30,741	4,810	--	1,880	37,431
	Lodgepole pine	1,298	116	--	--	1,414
	Limber pine	1,005	--	--	--	1,005
	Spruce-subalpine fir	8,623	--	--		8,623
	White fir	6,913	--	772		7,685
	Spruce	14,902	577	--		15,479
	Aspen	1,996	841	324	--	3,161
	Cottonwood	1,600	--	--	--	1,600
	All types	87,118	13,687	1,096	1,880	103,781
Nonindustrial private:						
	Douglas-fir	428,550	139,850	--	1,131	569,531
	Ponderosa pine	611,285	103,879	--	27,376	742,540
	Lodgepole pine	67,823	4,821	--	--	72,644
	Limber pine	41,772	--	--		41,772
	Spruce-subalpine fir	277,221	--	--		277,221
	White fir	129,127	14,876	16,135		160,138
	Spruce	585,568	8,111	1,826		595,505
	Aspen	66,809	40,084	9,998	--	116,891
	Cottonwood	35,710	5,511	--	--	41,221
	All types	2,243,865	317,132	27,959	28,507	2,617,463
Total:						
	Douglas-fir	448,590	147,193	--	1,131	596,914
	Ponderosa pine	642,026	108,689	--	29,256	779,971
	Lodgepole pine	69,121	4,937	--	--	74,058
	Limber pine	42,777	--	--	--	42,777
	Spruce-subalpine fir	285,844	--	--		285,844
	White fir	136,040	14,876	16,907		167,823
	Spruce	600,470	8,688	1,826		610,984
	Aspen	68,805	40,925	10,322	--	120,052
	Cottonwood	37,310	5,511	--	--	42,821
	All types	2,330,983	330,819	29,055	30,387	2,721,244

Table 19.--Net volume of growing stock on State and privately owned timberland by ownership class and species in Colorado's southern Front Range, 1983

Species	Ownership class		
	State	Nonindustrial private	Total
	- - - - - - - - - Thousand cubic feet - - - - - - - - -		
Douglas-fir	9,634	208,946	218,580
Ponderosa pine	13,551	276,775	290,326
Lodgepole pine	1,345	69,670	71,015
Whitebark pine	598	19,045	19,643
Limber pine	816	21,682	22,498
Subalpine fir	1,474	46,062	47,536
White fir	2,865	56,999	59,864
Engelmann spruce	6,481	222,886	229,367
Total softwoods	36,764	922,065	958,829
Aspen	2,347	74,192	76,539
Cottonwood	285	20,782	21,067
Total hardwoods	2,632	94,974	97,606
All species	39,396	1,017,039	1,056,435

Table 20.--Net volume of sawtimber (International ¼-inch rule) on State and privately owned timberland by ownership class and species in Colorado's southern Front Range, 1983

Species	Ownership class		
	State	Nonindustrial private	Total
	- - Thousand board feet, International ¼-inch rule - -		
Douglas-fir	35,831	808,524	844,355
Ponderosa pine	44,451	886,774	931,225
Lodgepole pine	1,197	67,467	68,664
Whitebark pine	1,580	63,013	64,593
Limber pine	2,365	84,077	86,442
Subalpine fir	2,160	78,992	81,152
White fir	9,404	160,253	169,657
Engelmann spruce	22,238	830,323	852,561
Total softwoods	119,226	2,979,423	3,098,649
Aspen	2,206	74,258	76,464
Cottonwood	1,299	41,818	43,117
Total hardwoods	3,505	116,076	119,581
All species	122,731	3,095,499	3,218,230

Table 21.--Net volume of sawtimber (Scribner rule) on State and privately owned timberland by ownership class and species in Colorado's southern Front Range, 1983

| Species | Ownership class | | Total |
	State	Nonindustrial private	
	- - - - - Thousand board feet, Scribner rule - - - - -		
Douglas-fir	30,182	683,209	713,391
Ponderosa pine	37,520	748,127	785,647
Lodgepole pine	1,057	57,974	59,031
Whitebark pine	1,320	52,879	54,199
Limber pine	2,020	72,142	74,162
Subalpine fir	1,874	67,884	69,758
White fir	7,997	136,161	144,158
Engelmann spruce	18,781	699,691	718,472
Total softwoods	100,751	2,518,067	2,618,818
Aspen	1,875	63,190	65,065
Cottonwood	1,155	36,206	37,361
Total hardwoods	3,030	99,396	102,426
All species	103,781	2,617,463	2,721,244

Table 22.--Net volume of growing stock on State and privately owned timberland by species and diameter class in Colorado's southern Front Range, 1983

Species	Diameter class (inches at breast height)													All classes
	5.0-6.9	7.0-8.9	9.0-10.9	11.0-12.9	13.0-14.9	15.0-16.9	17.0-18.9	19.0-20.9	21.0-22.9	23.0-24.9	25.0-26.9	27.0-28.9	29.0+	
	- - - - - - - - - - - - - - - - - - Thousand cubic feet - - - - - - - - - - - - - - - -													
Douglas-fir	14,272	32,030	20,302	22,873	32,923	35,039	18,535	14,655	15,517	5,724	3,560	859	2,291	218,580
Ponderosa pine	26,049	55,876	48,670	29,790	44,582	23,638	27,942	15,337	6,244	2,334	5,325	1,361	3,178	290,326
Lodgepole pine	35,671	17,448	7,789	5,583	4,524	--	--	--	--	--	--	--	--	71,015
■ pine	1,386	2,497	2,564	3,973	3,796	3,536	1,342	549	--	--	--	--	--	19,643
Limber pine	1,598	831	3,071	7,742	1,918	1,046	1,406	1,928	420	--	861	959	718	22,498
Subalpine fir	15,824	11,393	16,555	2,197	--	745	822	--	--	--	--	--	--	47,536
White fir	8,505	10,644	9,568	10,789	3,974	6,879	1,921	2,637	3,116	--	--	1,097	734	59,864
Engelmann spruce	11,629	31,202	28,040	57,491	32,130	27,246	19,387	9,243	4,454	1,679	6,866	--	--	229,367
Total softwoods	114,934	161,921	136,559	140,438	123,847	98,129	71,355	44,349	29,751	9,737	16,612	4,276	6,921	958,829
Aspen	24,719	22,232	13,756	8,718	4,210	2,904	--	--	--	--	--	--	--	76,539
Cottonwood	1,443	3,213	7,225	1,350	--	1,055	946	--	--	--	--	--	5,835	21,067
Total hardwoods	26,162	25,445	20,981	10,068	4,210	3,959	946	--	--	--	--	--	5,835	97,606
All species	141,096	187,366	157,540	150,506	128,057	102,088	72,301	44,349	29,751	9,737	16,612	4,276	12,756	1,056,435

Table 23.--Net volume of sawtimber (International ¼-inch rule) on State and privately owned timberland by species and diameter class in Colorado's southern Front Range, 1983

Species	Diameter class (inches at breast height)											
	9.0-10.9	11.0-12.9	13.0-14.9	15.0-16.9	17.0-18.9	19.0-20.9	21.0-22.9	23.0-24.9	25.0-26.9	27.0-28.9	29.0+	All classes
	- - - - - - - - - - - - - - - - - - - Thousand board feet, International ¼-inch rule - - - - - - - - - - - - - - - - -											- - - - -
Douglas-fir	67,791	103,375	162,248	178,285	97,196	80,540	84,993	31,930	19,776	4,923	13,298	844,355
Ponderosa pine	156,293	117,307	212,379	121,033	143,852	81,605	33,316	12,485	28,514	7,279	17,162	931,225
Lodgepole pine	23,397	23,528	21,739	--	--	--	--	--	--	--	--	68,664
Whitebark pine	7,755	15,643	15,731	16,258	6,518	2,688	--	--	--	--	--	64,593
Limber pine	10,983	31,104	8,243	4,451	6,873	8,987	2,116	--	4,669	5,097	3,919	86,442
Subalpine fir	63,571	9,873	--	3,672	4,036	--	--	--	--	--	--	81,152
White fir	31,209	46,948	17,861	32,223	8,590	11,522	13,364	--	--	4,634	3,306	169,657
Engelmann spruce	92,224	260,530	153,660	134,314	95,178	46,327	22,897	8,776	38,655	--	--	852,561
Total softwoods	453,223	608,308	591,861	490,236	362,243	231,669	156,686	53,191	91,614	21,933	37,685	3,098,649
Aspen	XXXX	40,992	20,598	14,874	--	--	--	--	--	--	--	76,464
Cottonwood	XXXX	6,871	--	5,178	4,491	--	--	--	--	--	26,577	43,117
Total hardwoods	XXXX	47,863	20,598	20,052	4,491	--	--	--	--	--	26,577	119,581
All species	453,223	656,171	612,459	510,288	366,734	231,669	156,686	53,191	91,614	21,933	64,262	3,218,230

Table 24.—Net volume of sawtimber (Scribner rule) on State and privately owned timberland by species and diameter class in Colorado's southern Front Range, 1983

Species	Diameter class (inches at breast height)											All classes
	9.0-10.9	11.0-12.9	13.0-14.9	15.0-16.9	17.0-18.9	19.0-20.9	21.0-22.9	23.0-24.9	25.0-26.9	27.0-28.9	29.0+	
	- - - - - - - - - - - - - - - Thousand board feet, Scribner rule - - - - - - - - - - - - - - -											
Douglas-fir	60,237	88,906	135,135	146,521	78,906	68,811	73,076	28,141	17,442	4,381	11,835	713,391
Ponderosa pine	118,979	94,585	181,703	105,435	125,617	71,898	29,414	11,048	25,268	6,451	15,249	785,647
Lodgepole pine	20,634	20,064	18,333	--	--	--	--	--	--	--	--	59,031
Whitebark pine	5,933	13,435	13,411	13,724	5,441	2,255	--	--	--	--	--	54,199
Limber pine	9,561	26,644	7,003	3,773	5,773	7,560	1,766	--	4,156	4,438	3,488	74,162
Subalpine fir	55,040	8,455	--	2,990	3,273	--	--	--	--	--	--	69,758
White fir	27,402	40,354	15,097	26,494	6,992	9,331	11,420	--	--	4,125	2,943	144,158
Engelmann spruce	82,003	222,050	127,693	109,717	77,241	37,784	19,874	7,708	34,402	--	--	718,472
Total softwoods	379,789	514,493	498,375	408,654	303,243	197,639	135,550	46,897	81,268	19,395	33,515	2,618,818
Aspen	XXXXX	35,128	17,386	12,551	--	--	--	--	--	--	--	65,065
Cottonwood	XXXXX	5,512	--	4,358	3,838	--	--	--	--	--	23,653	37,361
Total hardwoods	XXXXX	40,640	17,386	16,909	3,838	--	--	--	--	--	23,653	102,426
All species	379,789	555,133	515,761	425,563	307,081	197,639	135,550	46,897	81,268	19,395	57,168	2,721,244

Table 25. Net volume of timber on State and privately owned timberland by class of timber, and softwoods and hardwoods in Colorado's southern Front Range, 1983

Class of timber	Softwoods	Hardwoods	All classes
	Thousand cubic feet		
Sawtimber trees:			
Saw-log portion	593,991	19,387	613,378
Upper-stem portion	87,984	5,630	93,614
Total	681,975	25,017	706,992
Poletimber trees	276,854	72,589	349,443
All growing stock trees	958,829	97,606	1,056,435
Sound cull trees	1,769	--	1,769
Rotten cull trees	4,054	1,994	6,048
Salvable dead trees	49,933	7,194	57,127
All timber	1,014,585	106,794	1,121,379

Table 26.--Net volume of growing stock on State and privately owned timberland by forest type and species in Colorado's southern Front Range, 1983

Forest type	Species												
	Douglas-fir	Ponderosa pine	Lodgepole pine	Whitebark pine	Limber pine	Subalpine fir	White fir	Engelmann spruce	Total softwoods	Aspen	Cotton-wood	Total hardwoods	All species
	Thousand cubic feet												
Douglas-fir	143,980	11,933	4,625	3,325	10,000	1,130	18,806	11,615	205,414	7,076	--	7,076	212,490
Ponderosa pine	16,774	265,019	--	--	--	--	4,922	--	286,715	14,968	--	14,968	301,683
Lodgepole pine	--	--	66,390	--	--	1,528	--	7,066	74,984	696	--	696	75,680
Limber pine	2,320	--	--	--	7,563	--	2,668	--	12,551	3,909	--	3,909	16,460
Spruce-subalpine fir	19,711	--	--	14,542	4,515	35,533	--	32,581	106,882	--	--	--	106,882
White fir	22,215	7,096	--	--	420	--	27,567	--	57,298	7,347	--	7,347	64,645
Spruce	2,086	--	--	1,143	--	8,600	--	175,695	187,524	6,287	--	6,287	193,811
Aspen	11,494	5,019	--	633	--	745	5,901	2,410	26,202	36,256	--	36,256	62,458
Cottonwood	--	1,259	--	--	--	--	--	--	1,259	--	21,067	21,067	22,326
All types	218,580	290,326	71,015	19,643	22,498	47,536	59,864	229,367	958,829	76,539	21,067	97,606	1,056,435

Table 27.--Net volume of sawtimber (International ¼-inch rule) on State and privately owned timberland by forest type and species in Colorado's southern Front Range, 1983

Forest type	Species												
	Douglas-fir	Ponderosa pine	Lodgepole pine	Whitebark pine	Limber pine	Subalpine fir	White fir	Engelmann spruce	Total softwoods	Aspen	Cotton-wood	Total hardwoods	All species
	- - - - - - - - - - - - - - - - - Thousand board feet, International ¼-inch rule - - - - - - - - - - - - - - - -												
Douglas-fir	530,386	45,114	1,867	12,576	36,210	2,774	51,485	23,896	704,308	--	--	--	704,308
Ponderosa pine	69,280	821,858	--	--	--	--	13,428	--	904,566	23,412	--	23,412	927,978
Lodgepole pine	--	--	66,797	--	--	7,099	--	12,505	86,401	--	--	--	86,401
Limber pine	5,635	--	--	--	29,236	--	11,107	--	45,978	4,331	--	4,331	50,309
Spruce-subalpine fir	98,511	--	--	52,017	18,880	50,926	--	115,478	335,812	--	--	--	335,812
White fir	71,516	32,001	--	--	2,116	--	76,946	--	182,579	14,413	--	14,413	196,992
Spruce	11,251	--	--	--	--	16,682	--	691,400	719,333	7,256	--	7,256	726,589
Aspen	57,776	25,957	--	--	--	3,671	16,691	9,282	113,377	27,052	--	27,052	140,429
Cottonwood	--	6,295	--	--	--	--	--	9,282	6,295	--	43,117	43,117	49,412
All types	844,355	931,225	68,664	64,593	86,442	81,152	169,657	852,561	3,098,649	76,464	43,117	119,581	3,218,230

Table 28.--Net volume of sawtimber (Scribner rule) on State and privately owned timberland by forest type and species in Colorado's southern Front Range, 1983

Forest type	Species												
	Douglas-fir	Ponderosa pine	Lodgepole pine	Whitebark pine	Limber pine	Subalpine fir	White fir	Engelmann spruce	Total softwoods	Aspen	Cotton-wood	Total hardwoods	All species
	- - - - - - - - - - - - - - - - - Thousand board feet, Scribner rule - - - - - - - - - - - - - - - -												
Douglas-fir	448,740	38,535	1,473	10,668	31,414	2,451	43,225	20,408	596,914	--	--	--	596,914
Ponderosa pine	57,097	691,361	--	--	--	--	11,534	--	759,992	19,979	--	19,979	779,971
Lodgepole pine	--	--	57,558	--	--	6,004	--	10,496	74,058	--	--	--	74,058
Limber pine	4,873	--	--	--	24,890	--	9,252	--	39,015	3,762	--	3,762	42,777
Spruce-subalpine fir	83,712	--	--	43,531	16,092	43,697	--	98,812	285,844	--	--	--	285,844
White fir	60,542	27,684	--	--	1,766	--	65,639	--	155,631	12,192	--	12,192	167,823
Spruce	9,342	--	--	--	--	14,616	--	580,781	604,739	6,245	--	6,245	610,984

Table 29.--Net annual growth of growing stock on State and privately owned
          timberland by ownership class and species in Colorado's southern
          Front Range, 1982

Species	Ownership class		
	State	Nonindustrial private	Total
	- - - - - - - - Thousand cubic feet - - - - - - - -		
Douglas-fir	139	2,214	2,353
Ponderosa pine	250	4,760	5,010
Lodgepole pine	97	4,879	4,976
Whitebark pine	7	224	231
Limber pine	11	235	246
Subalpine fir	37	1,107	1,144
White fir	-20	374	354
Engelmann spruce	122	3,392	3,514
Total softwoods	643	17,185	17,828
Aspen	63	1,572	1,635
Cottonwood	3	752	755
Total hardwoods	66	2,324	2,390
All species	709	19,509	20,218

Table 30.--Net annual growth of sawtimber (International ¼-inch rule) on State
          and privately owned timberland by ownership class and species in
          Colorado's southern Front Range, 1982

Species	Ownership class		
	State	Nonindustrial private	Total
	- - Thousand board feet, International ¼-inch rule - -		
Douglas-fir	712	17,916	18,628
Ponderosa pine	1,187	23,112	24,299
Lodgepole pine	27	2,933	2,960
Whitebark pine	13	625	638
Limber pine	26	882	908
Subalpine fir	59	1,921	1,980
White fir	-109	-362	-471
Engelmann spruce	449	10,846	11,295
Total softwoods	2,364	57,873	60,237
Aspen	291	9,298	9,589
Cottonwood	16	621	637
Total hardwoods	307	9,919	10,226
All species	2,671	67,792	70,463

Table 31.--Net annual growth of sawtimber (Scribner rule) on State and
privately owned timberland by ownership class and species in
Colorado's southern Front Range, 1982

Species	Ownership class		
	State	Nonindustrial private	Total
	- - - - Thousand board feet, Scribner rule - - - -		
Douglas-fir	595	15,255	15,850
Ponderosa pine	988	19,243	20,231
Lodgepole pine	28	2,444	2,472
Whitebark pine	11	548	559
Limber pine	21	739	760
Subalpine fir	49	1,563	1,612
White fir	-96	-338	-434
Engelmann spruce	362	8,668	9,030
Total soft woods	1,958	48,122	50,080
Aspen	251	8,000	8,251
Cottonwood	14	563	577
Total hard woods	265	8,563	8,828
All species	2,223	56,685	58,908

Table 32.--Net annual growth of growing stock on State and privately owned timberland by species and diameter class in Colorado's southern Front Range, 1982

Species	Diameter class (inches at breast height)													
	5.0-6.9	7.0-8.9	9.0-10.9	11.0-12.9	13.0-14.9	15.0-16.9	17.0-18.9	19.0-20.9	21.0-22.9	23.0-24.9	25.0-26.9	27.0-28.9	29.0+	All classes
	- Thousand cubic feet -													
Douglas-fir	602	584	-147	264	405	424	180	81	-88	22	15	3	8	2,353
Ponderosa pine	1,075	1,450	851	559	498	-21	292	167	56	16	33	15	19	5,010
Lodgepole pine	4,002	682	189	73	30	--	--	--	--	--	--	--	--	4,976
Whitebark pine	61	41	36	43	24	17	5	4	--	--	--	--	--	231
Limber pine	64	15	32	73	23	5	7	10	1	--	5	8	3	246
Subalpine fir	428	268	379	48	--	15	6	--	--	--	--	--	--	1,144
White fir	233	261	-127	-70	-144	88	28	30	41	--	--	9	5	354
Engelmann spruce	667	635	611	758	284	210	188	90	36	13	22	--	--	3,514
Total softwoods	7,132	3,936	1,824	1,748	1,120	738	706	382	46	51	75	35	35	17,828
Aspen	1,234	488	-19	-174	79	27	--	--	--	--	--	--	--	1,635
Cottonwood	326	68	229	31	--	15	13	--	--	--	--	--	73	755
Total hardwoods	1,560	556	210	-143	79	42	13	--	--	--	--	--	73	2,390
All species	8,692	4,492	2,034	1,605	1,199	780	719	382	46	51	75	35	108	20,218

Table 33.--Net annual growth of sawtimber (International ¼-inch rule) on State and privately owned timberland by species and diameter class in Colorado's southern Front Range, 1982

Species	Diameter class (inches at breast height)											
	9.0-10.9	11.0-12.9	13.0-14.9	15.0-16.9	17.0-18.9	19.0-20.9	21.0-22.9	23.0-24.9	25.0-26.9	27.0-28.9	29.0+	All classes
	Thousand board feet, International ¼-inch rule											
Douglas-fir	10,802	1,680	2,329	2,421	1,022	478	-402	137	96	17	48	18,628
Ponderosa pine	14,803	3,220	2,899	27	1,656	930	308	90	178	81	107	24,299
Lodgepole pine	2,362	406	192	--	--	--	--	--	--	--	--	2,960
Whitebark pine	120	238	127	103	27	23	--	--	--	--	--	638
Limber pine	173	388	123	31	40	58	2	--	28	48	17	908
Subalpine fir	1,603	270	--	76	31	--	--	--	--	--	--	1,980
White fir	-623	-124	-594	408	112	115	165	--	--	45	25	-471
Engelmann spruce	2,100	4,519	1,617	1,159	974	485	218	79	144	--	--	11,295
Total softwoods	31,340	10,597	6,693	4,225	3,862	2,089	291	306	446	191	197	60,237

Table 34.--Net annual growth of sawtimbe r(Scribner rule) on State and privately owned timberland by species and diameter class in Colorado's southern Front Range, 1982

Species	Diameter class (inches at breast height)											All classes
	9.0-10.9	11.0-12.9	13.0-14.9	15.0-16.9	17.0-18.9	19.0-20.9	21.0-22.9	23.0-24.9	25.0-26.9	27.0-28.9	29.0+	
	- Thousand board feet, Scribner rule -											
Douglas-fir	9,600	1,315	1,831	1,904	804	412	-297	135	88	15	43	15,850
Ponderosa pine	11,702	2,880	2,596	55	1,483	832	275	81	159	72	96	20,231
Lodgepole pine	1,975	337	160	--	--	--	--	--	--	--	--	2,472
Whitebark pine	128	197	105	85	25	19	--	--	--	--	--	559
Limber pine	144	322	101	25	33	48	2	--	25	45	15	760
Subalpine fir	1,316	212	--	60	24	--	--	--	--	--	--	1,612
White fir	-486	-147	-520	319	87	90	158	--	--	43	22	-434
Engelmann spruce	1,858	3,465	1,235	885	766	401	214	77	129	--	--	9,030
Total softwoods	26,237	8,581	5,508	3,333	3,222	1,802	352	293	401	175	176	50,080
Aspen	XXXX	7,749	376	126	--	--	--	--	--	--	--	8,251
Cottonwood	XXXX	151	--	62	49	--	--	--	--	--	315	577
Total hardwoods	XXXX	7,900	376	188	49	--	--	--	--	--	315	8,828
All species	26,237	16,481	5,884	3,521	3,271	1,802	352	293	401	175	491	58,908

Table 35.--Annual mortality of growing stock on State and privately owned
timberland by ownership class and species in Colorado's southern
Front Range, 1982

Species	Ownership class		
	State	Nonindustrial private	Total
	- - - - - - - - Thousand cubic feet - - - - - - - -		
Douglas-fir	43	1,000	1,043
Ponderosa pine	25	622	647
White fir	78	913	991
Engelmann spruce	--	727	727
Total softwoods	146	3,262	3,408
Aspen	--	594	594
Total hardwoods	--	594	594
All species	146	3,856	4,002

Table 36.--Annual mortality of sawtimber (International ¼-inch rule) on State
and privately owned timberland by ownership class and species in
Colorado's southern Front Range, 1982

Species	Ownership class		
	State	Nonindustrial private	Total
	- Thousand board feet, International ¼-inch rule -		
Douglas-fir	76	2,820	2,896
Ponderosa pine	100	1,932	2,032
White fir	262	2,923	3,185
Engelmann spruce	--	3,511	3,511
Total softwoods	438	11,186	11,624
Aspen	--	1,463	1,463
Total hardwoods	--	1,463	1,463
All species	438	12,649	13,087

Table 37.--Annual mortality of sawtimber (Scribner rule) on State and privately owned timberland by ownership class and species in Colorado's southern Front Range, 1982

Species	Ownership class		
	State	Nonindustrial private	Total
	- - - - Thousand board feet, Scribner rule - - - -		
Douglas-fir	68	2,476	2,544
Ponderosa pine	88	1,696	1,784
White fir	225	2,547	2,772
Engelmann spruce	--	2,911	2,911
Total softwoods	381	9,630	10,011
Aspen	--	1,256	1,256
Total hardwoods	--	1,256	1,256
All species	381	10,886	11,267

Table 38.--Annual mortality of growing stock on State and privately owned timberland by species and diameter class in Colorado's southern Front Range, 1982

Species	Diameter class (inches at breast height)													
	5.0-6.9	7.0-8.9	9.0-10.9	11.0-12.9	13.0-14.9	15.0-16.9	17.0-18.9	19.0-20.9	21.0-22.9	23.0-24.9	25.0-26.9	27.0-28.9	29.0+	All classes
	- - - - - - - - - - - - - - - - - - Thousand cubic feet - - - - - - - - - - - - - - - - - -													
Douglas-fir	--	245	543	71	--	--	--	--	184	--	--	--	--	1,043
Ponderosa pine	40	105	252	--	--	250	--	--	--	--	--	--	--	647
White fir	178	72	314	246	181	--	--	--	--	--	--	--	--	991
Engelmann spruce	--	--	--	380	190	157	--	--	--	--	--	--	--	727
Total softwoods	218	422	1,109	697	371	407	--	--	184	--	--	--	--	3,408
Aspen	XXXXX	--	286	308	--	--	--	--	--	--	--	--	--	594
Total hardwoods	XXXXX	--	286	308	--	--	--	--	--	--	--	--	--	594
All species	218	422	1,395	1,005	371	407	--	--	184	--	--	--	--	4,002

Table 39.--Annual mortality of sawtimber (International ¼-inch rule) on State and privately owned timberland by species and diameter class in Colorado's southern Front Range, 1982

Species	Diameter class (inches at breast height)											
	9.0-10.9	11.0-12.9	13.0-14.9	15.0-16.9	17.0-18.9	19.0-20.9	21.0-22.9	23.0-24.9	25.0-26.9	27.0-28.9	29.0+	All classes
	- - - - - - - - - - - - - - Thousand board feet, International ¼-inch rule - - - - - - - - - - - - - -											
Douglas-fir	1,628	271	--	--	--	--	997	--	--	--	--	2,896
Ponderosa pine	753	--	--	1,279	--	--	--	--	--	--	--	2,032
White fir	1,302	1,103	780	--	--	--	--	--	--	--	--	3,185
Engelmann spruce	--	1,809	935	767	--	--	--	--	--	--	--	3,511
Total softwoods	3,683	3,183	1,715	2,046	--	--	997	--	--	--	--	11,624
Aspen	XXXXX	1,463	--	--	--	--	--	--	--	--	--	1,463
Total hardwoods	XXXXX	1,463	--	--	--	--	--	--	--	--	--	1,463
All species	3,683	4,646	1,715	2,046	--	--	997	--	--	--	--	13,087

Table 40.--Annual mortality of sawtimber (Scribner rule) on State and privately owned timberland by species and diameter class in Colorado's southern Front Range, 1982

Species	Diameter class (inches at breast height)											
	9.0-10.9	11.0-12.9	13.0-14.9	15.0-16.9	17.0-18.9	19.0-20.9	21.0-22.9	23.0-24.9	25.0-26.9	27.0-28.9	29.0+	All classes
	- - - - - - - - - - - - - - Thousand board feet, Scribner rule - - - - - - - - - - - - - -											

Table 41.--Annual mortality of growing stock on State and privately owned timberland by cause of death and species in Colorado's southern Front Range, 1982

Species	Cause of death								
	Insects	Disease	Fire	Animal	Weather	Suppression	Logging	Unknown[1]	Total
	- - - - - - - - - - - - - - - Thousand cubic feet -								
Douglas-fir	--	133	--	--	910	--	--	--	1,043
Ponderosa pine	395	252	--	--	--	--	--	--	647
White fir	387	--	--	--	308	57	58	181	991
Engelmann spruce	--	157	--	--	--	--	--	570	727
Total softwoods	782	542	--	--	1,218	57	58	751	3,408
Aspen	--	171	--	--	--	--	--	423	594
Total hardwoods	--	171	--	--	--	--	--	423	594
All species	782	713	--	--	1,218	57	58	1,174	4,002

[1]Because many destructive agents often attack trees in concert or in succession, it is often difficult to identify the actual causal agent. When the primary cause of death cannot be precisely determined, it is listed as unknown.

Table 42.--Annual mortality of sawtimber (International ¼-inch rule) on State and privately owned timberland by cause of death and species in Colorado's southern Front Range, 1982

Species	Cause of death								
	Insects	Disease	Fire	Animal	Weather	Suppression	Logging	Unknown[1]	Total
	- - - - - - - - - - Thousand board feet, International ¼-inch rule - - - - - - - - - - - -								
Douglas-fir	--	272	--	--	2,624	--	--	--	2,896
Ponderosa pine	1,279	753	--	--	--	--	--	--	2,032
White fir	1,302	--	--	--	1,103	--	--	780	3,185
Engelmann spruce	--	767	--	--	--	--	--	2,744	3,511
Total softwoods	2,581	1,792	--	--	3,727	--	--	3,524	11,624
Aspen	--	838	--	--	--	--	--	625	1,463
Total hardwoods	--	838	--	--	--	--	--	625	1,463
All species	2,581	2,630	--	--	3,727	--	--	4,149	13,087

[1]Because many destructive agents often attack trees in concert or in succession, it is often difficult to identify the actual causal agent. When the primary cause of death cannot be precisely determined, it is listed as unknown.

Table 43.--Annual mortality of sawtimber (Scribner rule) on State and privately owned timberland by cause of death and species in Colorado's southern Front Range, 1982

					Thousand board feet, Scribner rule				
Douglas-fir	--	242	--	--	2,302	--	--	--	2,54
Ponderosa pine	1,113	671	--	--	--	--	--	--	1,78
White fir	1,159	--	--	--	946	--	--	667	2,77
Engelmann spruce	--	627	--	--	--	--	--	2,284	2,91

Total softwoods

Aspen

Total hardwoods

All s

[1]Because many destructive agents often attack trees in concert or in succession, it is often difficult to identify the actual causal agent. When the primary cause of death cannot be precisely determined, it is listed as unknown.

Table 44.--Area of State and privately owned woodland by ownership class and forest type in Colorado's southern Front Range, 1983

Forest type	Ownership class		
	State	Nonindustrial private	Total
	- - - - - - - - - Acres - - - - - - - - -		
Pinyon-juniper	60,471	733,108	793,579
Juniper	18,231	191,381	209,612
Total woodland softwoods	78,702	924,489	1,003,191
Oak	1,824	57,569	59,393
Other west hardwoods	229	9,504	9,733
Total woodland hardwoods	2,053	67,073	69,126
All types	80,755	991,562	1,072,317

Table 45.--Net volume of State and privately owned woodland by ownership class and species in Colorado's southern Front Range, 1983

Species	Ownership class		Total
	State	Nonindustrial private	
	- - - - - - - - Thousand cubic feet - - - - - - -		
Douglas-fir	--	--	--
Ponderosa pine	9	111	120
Aspen	--	--	--
Pinyon/juniper	26,166	301,383	327,549
Woodland hardwoods	764	9,463	10,227
All species	26,939	310,957	337,896

Table 46.--Net annual growth of State and privately owned woodland by ownership class and species in Colorado's southern Front Range, 1982

Species	Ownership class		Total
	State	Nonindustrial private	
	- - - - - - - - Thousand cubic feet - - - - - - - -		
Douglas-fir	--	--	--
Ponderosa pine	(^{1})	2	2
Aspen	--	--	--
Pinyon/juniper	367	4,268	4,635
Woodland hardwoods	-13	-78	-91
All species	354	4,192	4,546

^{1}Less than 500 cubic feet.

Table 47.--Annual mortality of State and privately owned woodland by ownership class and species in Colorado's southern Front Range, 1982

Species	Ownership class		Total
	State	Nonindustrial private	
	- - - - - - - Thousand cubic feet - - - - - - -		
Douglas-fir			
Ponderosa pine	--	--	--
Aspen	--	--	--
Pinyon/juniper	2	69	71
Woodland hardwoods	35	341	376
All species	37	410	447

Table 48.--Area of State and privately owned timberland by county and ownership class in Colorado's southern Front Range, 1983

County	Ownership class		
	State	Nonindustrial private	Total
	- - - - - - - - - - Acres - - - - - - - - - - - - -		
Chaffee	3,234	32,883	36,117
Costilla	--	189,272	189,272
Custer	3,316	76,721	80,037
Fremont	10,513	75,596	86,109
Huerfano	5,441	100,586	106,027
Las Animas	15,684	368,057	383,741
Pueblo	4,623	62,536	67,159
Total	42,811	905,651	948,462

Table 49.--Net volume of growing stock on State and privately owned timberland by county and ownership class in Colorado's southern Front Range, 1983

County	Ownership class		
	State	Nonindustrial private	Total
	- - - - - - - - - Thousand cubic feet - - - - - - - -		
Chaffee	4,114	38,360	42,474
Costilla	--	309,373	309,373
Custer	3,776	87,736	91,512
Fremont	10,358	66,451	76,809
Huerfano	5,791	103,255	109,046
Las Animas	12,862	360,051	372,913
Pueblo	2,495	51,813	54,308
Total	39,396	1,017,039	1,056,435

Table 50.--Net volume of sawtimber (International ¼-inch rule) on State and privately owned timberland by county and ownership class in Colorado's southern Front Range, 1983

County	Ownership class		
	State	Nonindustrial private	Total
	- - Thousand board feet, International ¼-inch rule - -		
Chaffee	13,428	118,396	131,824
Costilla	--	892,199	892,199
Custer	12,133	274,745	286,878
Fremont	28,434	185,743	214,177
Huerfano	17,316	318,423	335,739
Las Animas	41,925	1,142,518	1,184,443
Pueblo	9,495	163,475	172,970
Total	122,731	3,095,499	3,218,230

Table 51.--Net volume of sawtimber (Scribner rule) on State and privately owned timberland by county and ownership class in Colorado's southern Front Range, 1983

County	Ownership class		
	State	Nonindustrial private	Total
	- - - - - Thousand board feet, Scribner rule - - - - -		
Chaffee	11,328	99,993	111,321
Costilla	--	756,854	756,854
Custer	10,251	232,179	242,430
Fremont	24,156	157,659	181,815
Huerfano	14,632	269,070	283,702
Las Animas	35,322	963,141	998,463
Pueblo	8,092	138,567	146,659
Total	103,781	2,617,463	2,721,244

Table 52.--Net annual growth of growing stock on State and privately owned timberland by county and ownership class in Colorado's southern Front Range, 1982

County	Ownership class		
	State	Nonindustrial private	Total
	- - - - - - - - Thousand cubic feet - - - - - - - - -		
Chaffee	73	778	851
Costilla	--	6,504	6,504
Custer	74	1,680	1,754
Fremont	186	1,307	1,493
Huerfano	141	2,315	2,456
Las Animas	193	5,875	6,068
Pueblo	42	1,050	1,092
Total	709	19,509	20,218

Table 53.--Net annual growth of sawtimber (International ¼-inch rule) on State and privately owned timberland by county and ownership class in Colorado's southern Front Range, 1982

County	Ownership class		
	State	Nonindustrial private	Total
	- - Thousand board feet, International ¼-inch rule - -		
Chaffee	544	4,572	5,116
Costilla	--	18,209	18,209
Custer	362	9,611	9,973
Fremont	282	2,087	2,369
Huerfano	630	11,743	12,373
Las Animas	579	15,860	16,439
Pueblo	274	5,710	5,984
Total	2,671	67,792	70,463

43

Table 54.--Net annual growth of sawtimber (Scribner rule) on State and
privately owned timberland by county and ownership class in
Colorado's southern Front Range, 1982

County	Ownership class		
	State	Nonindustrial private	Total
	- - - - - Thousand board feet, Scribner rule - - - - -		
Chaffee	451	3,802	4,253
Costilla	--	15,179	15,179
Custer	303	8,037	8,340
Fremont	232	1,749	1,981
Huerfano	512	9,602	10,114
Las Animas	504	13,603	14,107
Pueblo	221	4,713	4,934
Total	2,223	56,685	58,908

Table 55.--Annual mortality of growing stock on State and privately owned
timberland by county and ownership class in Colorado's southern
Front Range, 1982

County	Ownership class		
	State	Nonindustrial private	Total
	- - - - - - - - Thousand cubic feet - - - - - - - - -		
Chaffee	12	110	122
Costilla	--	1,875	1,875
Custer	13	339	352
Fremont	68	411	479
Huerfano	16	288	304
Las Animas	23	637	660
Pueblo	14	196	210
Total	146	3,856	4,002

Table 56.--Annual mortality of sawtimber (International ¼-inch rule) on State
and privately owned timberland by county and ownership class in
Colorado's southern Front Range, 1982

County	Ownership class		
	State	Nonindustrial private	Total
	- - Thousand board feet, International ¼-inch rule - -		
Chaffee	33	304	337
Costilla	--	6,952	6,952
Custer	30	859	889
Fremont	261	1,626	1,887
Huerfano	44	759	803
Las Animas	57	1,756	1,813
Pueblo	13	393	406
Total	438	12,649	13,087

Table 57.--Annual mortality of sawtimber (Scribner rule) on State and privately
        owned timberland by county and ownership class in Colorado's
        southern Front Range, 1982

County	Ownership class		
	State	Nonindustrial private	Total
	- - - - - Thousand board feet, Scribner rule - - - - -		
Chaffee	29	266	295
Costilla	--	5,887	5,887
Custer	26	754	780
Fremont	225	1,406	1,631
Huerfano	39	667	706
Las Animas	51	1,563	1,614
Pueblo	11	343	354
Total	381	10,886	11,267

Table 58.--Area of State and privately owned woodland by county and ownership
        class in Colorado's southern Front Range, 1983

County	Ownership class		
	State	Nonindustrial private	Total
	- - - - - - - - - - - Acres - - - - - - - - - - -		
Chaffee	1,118	18,851	19,969
Costilla	--	82,241	82,241
Custer	501	16,122	16,623
Fremont	14,384	112,298	126,682
Huerfano	7,988	131,176	139,164
Las Animas	48,316	564,746	613,062
Pueblo	8,448	66,128	74,576
Total	80,755	991,562	1,072,317

Table 59.--Net volume of State and privately owned woodland by county and
        ownership class in Colorado's southern Front Range, 1983

County	Ownership class		
	State	Nonindustrial private	Total
	- - - - - - - - - Thousand cubic feet - - - - - - - -		
Chaffee	560	7,115	7,675
Costilla	--	21,549	21,549
Custer	91	4,989	5,080
Fremont	6,518	50,343	56,861
Huerfano	3,461	53,681	57,142
Las Animas	13,366	149,947	163,313
Pueblo	2,943	23,333	26,276
Total	26,939	310,957	337,896

Table 60.--Net annual growth of State and privately owned woodland by county and ownership class in Colorado's southern Front Range, 1982

County	Ownership class		Total
	State	Nonindustrial private	
	- - - - - - - - Thousand cubic feet - - - - - - - -		
Chaffee	9	99	108
Costilla	--	273	273
Custer	1	79	80
Fremont	67	455	522
Huerfano	52	818	870
Las Animas	183	2,125	2,308
Pueblo	42	343	385
Total	354	4,192	4,546

Table 61.--Annual mortality of State and privately owned woodland by county and ownership class in Colorado's southern Front Range, 1982

County	Ownership class		Total
	State	Nonindustrial private	
	- - - - - - - - Thousand cubic feet - - - - - - - -		
Chaffee	(^{1})	6	6
Costilla	--	41	41
Custer	(^{1})	3	3
Fremont	34	332	366
Huerfano	1	8	9
Las Animas	1	15	16
Pueblo	1	5	6
Total	37	410	447

[1]Less than 500 cubic feet.

Conner, Roger C; Pawley, William T. 1987. Colorado's southern Front Range: forest statistics for State and private land, 1983. Resour. Bull. INT-43. Ogden, UT: U.S. Department of Agriculture, Forest Service, Intermountain Research Station. 46 p.

Presents land area, timberland area, woodland area, timber inventory, and growth and mortality data for seven counties in Colorado's southern Front Range. Information and statistical tables are based on Forest Survey data collected from 1982 and 1983 and cover State and private resources.

KEYWORDS: timberland, woodland, growing-stock volume, net annual growth, round-wood harvest, fuelwood harvest

INTERMOUNTAIN RESEARCH STATION

The Intermountain Research Station provides scientific knowledge and technology to improve management, protection, and use of the forests and rangelands of the Intermountain West. Research is designed to meet the needs of National Forest managers, Federal and State agencies, industry, academic institutions, public and private organizations, and individuals. Results of research are made available through publications, symposia, workshops, training sessions, and personal contacts.

The Intermountain Research Station territory includes Montana, Idaho, Utah, Nevada, and western Wyoming. Eighty-five percent of the lands in the Station area, about 231 million acres, are classified as forest or rangeland. They include grasslands, deserts, shrublands, alpine areas, and forests. They provide fiber for forest industries, minerals and fossil fuels for energy and industrial development, water for domestic and industrial consumption, forage for livestock and wildlife, and recreation opportunities for millions of visitors.

Several Station units conduct research in additional western States, or have missions that are national or international in scope.

Station laboratories are located in:

Boise, Idaho

Bozeman, Montana (in cooperation with Montana State University)

Logan, Utah (in cooperation with Utah State University)

Missoula, Montana (in cooperation with the University of Montana)

Moscow, Idaho (in cooperation with the University of Idaho)

Ogden, Utah

Provo, Utah (in cooperation with Brigham Young University)

Reno, Nevada (in cooperation with the University of Nevada)